VIOLIN

MAKING 🎵 MUSIC

KATE RIGGS

CREATIVE ◆ EDUCATION

PUBLISHED *by* Creative Education

P.O. Box 227, Mankato, Minnesota 56002

Creative Education is an imprint of The Creative Company

www.thecreativecompany.us

DESIGN AND PRODUCTION *by* Ellen Huber

ART DIRECTION *by* Rita Marshall

PRINTED *in the* United States of America

PHOTOGRAPHS *by*
Alamy (Colin Crisford), Corbis (Hill Street Studios/Blend
Images, Mike Kemp/Tetra Images, Lebrecht Music & Arts),
Dreamstime (Christopher Halloran), Getty Images
(Ethan Miller, Kyu Oh), iStockphoto (Evgeniy Gorbunov,
Martin Huber, Ela Kwasniewski, David H. Lewis, pixhook,
pixitive, ARPAD RADOCZY, Vladimir Tarasov, tunart,
wbgorex), Shutterstock (dean bertoncelj, Marie C. Fields,
isak55, Dan Kosmayer, Ela Kwasniewski, Blank Michael,
nobeastsofierce, Fedorov Oleksiy, lev radin, Dmitry Skutin,
Stokkete, Evlakhov Valeriy, vvoe, wacpan), SuperStock
(Exactostock), Veer (suljo)

LIBRARY OF CONGRESS
CATALOGING-IN-PUBLICATION DATA
Riggs, Kate.
Violin / Kate Riggs.
p. cm. — (Making music)
SUMMARY: *A primary prelude to the violin, including what*
the string instrument looks and sounds like, basic instructions on
how to play it, and the kinds of music that feature it.
Includes bibliographical references and index.

ISBN 978-1-60818-371-5
1. Violin—Juvenile literature. 1. Title.

ML800.R54 2013
787.2—DC23   2013009500

FIRST EDITION
9 8 7 6 5 4 3 2 1

TABLE OF CONTENTS

WHEN YOU HEAR A VIOLIN

A bright summer day.

A warm cookie melting in your hand.

Cars rushing through traffic.

What do you think of when you hear a violin?

A freshly baked cookie can be soft and gooey.
Sunshine and stillness are calming.

THE STRING FAMILY

Musical instruments that sound and look alike belong

to a "family." Violins are members of the string family.

They have four strings. The strings **vibrate**

when you pluck them or draw a **bow** across them.

Thinner strings are pulled tighter to make higher sounds.

Thicker strings make lower, deeper sounds.

A violin's strings cross a curved, wooden piece called a bridge.

guitar

banjo

mandolin

ukulele

sitar

lute

harp

violin

viola

cello

double bass

The f-holes help aim the sound as it comes out of the violin.

PARTS OF A VIOLIN

A violin is made of wood. Its body has parts

just like yours. The violin has a waist in

the middle, a long neck on top, and a back.

The sound bounces around inside the wooden body.

It comes out holes near the waist that

are shaped like the letter *f*.

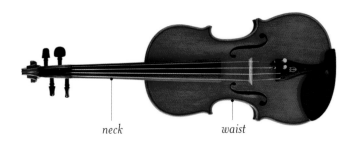

neck   waist

STRINGS AND PEGS

The "head" of the violin is called the scroll.

There are four pegs in the peg box near the scroll.

The strings are wrapped around the pegs.

The pegs turn to make the strings tighter or looser.

This **tunes** the instrument.

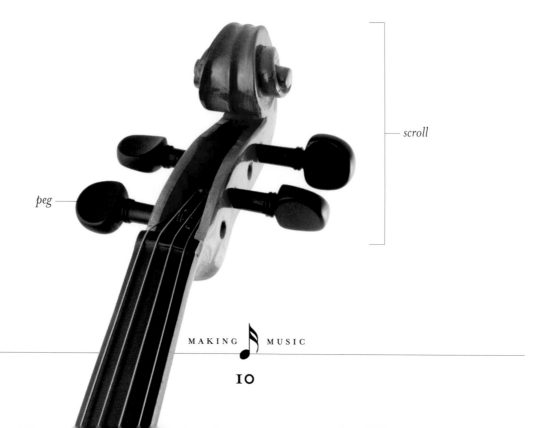

peg

scroll

The sides of a violin
scroll spiral in to make
a pretty curve.

Young children learn to play with a smaller violin and bow.

SIZES OF VIOLINS

Full-size violins are two feet (61 cm) long.

There are one-quarter, one-half,

and three-quarter violins, too.

These are smaller violins that fit smaller hands.

No matter what size they are, all violins have the same parts.

PLAYING THE VIOLIN

The end of the violin rests on your left shoulder

and under your face, near your chin.

You can sit down or stand when playing violin.

You curl the fingers of your left hand

around the neck to play notes on the strings.

You hold the bow in your right hand.

Your left thumb goes behind the neck, while the fingers are on top of the fingerboard.

A violinist draws the bow across the strings to make sound.

Some people still play viols called viola da gambas today.

EARLY VIOLINS

People started playing violins in Italy around 1550.

Before that, people played instruments called viols.

Viols usually had six strings.

They were shorter than violins.

The sound holes on a viol were shaped like the letter c.

VIOLIN MUSIC

The violin is an important instrument in

orchestras (*OR-keh-struhz*). It is part of the string section

with bigger instruments called violas (*vee-OH-lahz*),

cellos (*CHEH-lohz*), and double basses.

A violinist who plays by herself is a soloist. Many people

like to play violin in small groups called **string quartets**.

Violinists can either play with others (left) or by themselves (pictured).

A solo violinist often plays from memory and does not need to look at music.

A VIOLINIST PLAYS

A violinist stands in front of the orchestra.

She draws the bow across the strings.

The violin sings a gentle song.

Everyone smiles, and the violin sets the mood!

MEET A VIOLINIST

Joshua Bell was born in 1967 and grew up in

Bloomington, Indiana. He has played violin since he was four years

old. Joshua played with a famous orchestra when he was 14.

He started **recording** *music when he was 18.*

Now he has made more than 40 CDs! Joshua plays

a violin that is 300 years old. It was made by

a man named Antonio Stradivari (strad-uh-VAIR-ee).

Joshua Bell travels around the world to play his violin for people.

GLOSSARY

bow: *a wooden rod with horsehairs used to play a string instrument*

recording: *making a CD or tape of something that can be played later*

string quartets: *groups made up of four string instruments (two violins, a viola, and a cello)*

tunes: *fixes the pitch, or sound, of an instrument*

vibrate: *to shake or move up and down rapidly*

READ MORE

Ganeri, Anita. *Stringed Instruments.*
North Mankato, Minn.: Smart Apple Media, 2012.

Levine, Robert. *The Story of the Orchestra.*
New York: Black Dog & Leventhal, 2001.

Storey, Rita. *The Violin and Other Stringed Instruments.*
North Mankato, Minn.: Smart Apple Media, 2010.

WEBSITES

Dallas Symphony Orchestra Kids
http://www.dsokids.com/default.aspx
Listen to the sounds a violin makes, play games, and make your own instrument.

San Francisco Orchestra Kids
http:www.sfskids.org/templates/home.asp?pageid=1
Learn more about orchestra instruments and make your own songs in the Music Lab.

Every effort has been made to ensure that these sites are suitable for children, that they have educational value, and that they contain no inappropriate material. However, because of the nature of the Internet, it is impossible to guarantee that these sites will remain active indefinitely or that their contents will not be altered.

INDEX